Martin Leman's
PAINTED CATS

Leonardo

Martin Leman's
PAINTED CATS

PELHAM BOOKS

$\mathcal{I}$ love cats because I love my home, and little by little they become its visible soul. A kind of active silence emanates from these furry beasts who appear deaf to orders, to appeals, to reproaches, and who move in a completely royal authority through the network of our acts, retaining only those that intrigue or comfort them.

Jean Cocteau

PELHAM BOOKS

Published by the Penguin Group
27 Wrights Lane, London W8 5TZ, England
Viking Penguin Inc., 40 West 23rd Street, New York, New York 10010, USA
Penguin Books Australia Ltd, Ringwood, Victoria, Australia
Penguin Books Canada Ltd, 2801 John Street, Markham, Ontario, Canada L3R 1B4
Penguin Books (NZ) Ltd, 182–190 Wairau Road, Auckland 10, New Zealand

Penguin Books Ltd. Registered Offices: Harmondsworth, Middlesex, England

First published 1988

Copyright © Jill and Martin Leman 1988

Research and design by Jill Leman

Printed and bound in Italy by Olivotto
Typeset by Goodfellow & Egan, Cambridge

A CIP catalogue record for this book is available from the British Library.

Claudius

Martin Leman

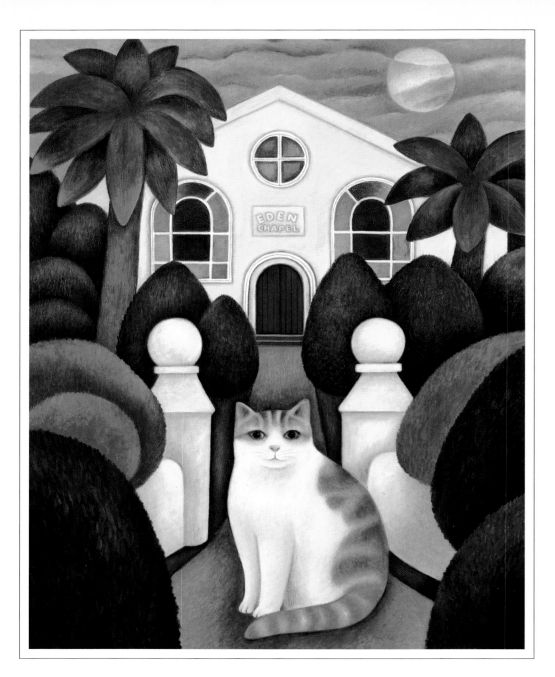

Tittlebat and Tavy

Tittlebat is only too sociable both indoors and out. When I settle myself before the fire with a book or newspaper he jumps up on my lap and insists on being petted; pushes the book away with his beautiful sleek head and nuzzles his nose into my hand again and again, and only consents to be quiet when I have given him the amount of attention that he considers his due. One day I had to go to the Rectory as it was getting dark, and did not know that he was following me. The way is across the lawn and through a region of Oaks and Hollies, then through the frame yard and all the length of the kitchen garden, past some Quince trees and out into the main road by the gardener's cottage. It is not far beyond that to the Rectory. When I came back it was quite dark. Passing the Quince trees I heard a disturbance in one of them, and something scrambled to the ground. I thought it was some neighbour's cock or hen gone to roost in the tree, but the thing said May-ow, and I knew my dear Tittlebat's voice. He had followed me down and got up into the Quince to wait till I came back.

Tavy is very fond of that place just at the top of the steps opposite the door of the sitting-room to the garden. He likes to sit there when he knows I am near him inside, and keeps an eye on the wood close by, where there are always some objects of interest, if not in sight at least within hearing. He is red tabby and white. He does not come with me so much in the garden as the others, but indoors he is my most constant companion of all. His fur is deliciously soft and fine, and he has dainty pretty ways, quite little ladyways, we always say. He has one odd trick that I do not remember having seen in any other cat. He puffs out his tail when he is pleased – usually a short-haired cat puffs out his tail only when he is frightened, or angry, or fighting. But Tavy makes a beautiful tail when we are playing together, and he is quite pleased with himself and me. On the rare occasions when he walks with me in the garden – he is jealous, and will never come if any other cat is present, he makes a beautiful tail and walks in a very odd way – a sort of waddling strut; we call it Tavy's ingratiating waddle; purring hard all the time and expecting a great deal of praise and attention.

Gertrude Jekyll

My Cats

When the cat family totalled fourteen my wife, abetted by my mother-in-law, insisted that something should be done about it. At about this time I met that great friend of cats, Mr Louis Wain, who told me that he housed over forty! In vain I pointed this out to my wife. She repeated firmly that something must be done.

By this time kittens had been supplied to all the people we knew who wanted them. At best I could only hope to dispose of kittens singly and at intervals, and meanwhile the said kittens were growing up. Some of them at least would have families of their own by the time new homes had been found for them. We were in a vicious circle, with the supply always overtaking the demand.

Then, one day, passing through one of the big department stores, I chanced to stop by the Animal Department. It suddenly occurred to me that here might be an opening for kittens in wholesale quantities. I made discreet enquiries, hurried home, commandeered the baby's pram (my wife being out) and sent off half a dozen. It took me a long time to pick them out, not so much because I had to choose them impartially and with due regard to maternal requirements, but because I simply hated to let them go.

When the pram returned empty I was both relieved and disappointed. The woman in the Animal Department had welcomed them, I gathered, their stock of kittens being low. But in future would I please supply more gentlemen kittens than ladies. In future! I thought it advisable to wait a week or so before sending the second batch. With one exception, a rather less beautiful female for whom I luckily found another home, these were also accepted and I was able to look my wife and mother-in-law in the face again.

Michael Joseph

Two White Kittens

Rufus

Beatrix Potter's Journal

Sunday, January 27 1884 – There was another story in the paper a week or so since. A gentleman had a favourite cat whom he taught to sit at the dinner table where it behaved very well. He was in the habit of putting any scraps he left on to the cat's plate. One day puss did not take his place punctually, but presently appeared with two mice, one of which it placed on its master's plate, the other on its own.

Saturday, March 28 1885 – There are signs that the domestic animals are revolting. From Holborn comes the news that one Mr Ashton, returning home, discovered his black tom had two visitors in the passage, whom Mr Ashton proceeded to eject, but all three set on him, and after a violent struggle Mr Ashton was driven precipitously out at the front door, and fell into the arms of two policemen who took him to the hospital.

Wednesday, September 12 1894 – When passing Twizel in the train I saw an absurd sight, a black cat and a hedgehog in a field. The cat was retreating, lifting its paws up, but turned and again approached the enemy with its tail on end. I should very much have liked to see the next round. It was a very large hedgehog and quite unconcerned.

Tuesday, January 7 1896 – The sweetest spectacle I have lately seen, the Store's cat, its paws folded under its white chest, its ears and white whiskers laid back, ignoring the roar of the Haymarket, in a new red morocco collar, couchant in a pile of biscuit canisters.

Séraphita

Séraphita was of a dreamy and contemplative disposition. She would remain for hours on a cushion, wide awake and following with her eyes, with intensest attention, sights invisible to ordinary mortals. She liked to be petted, but returned caresses in a very reserved way, and only in the case of persons whom she honoured with her approbation, a most difficult thing to obtain. She was fond of luxury, and we were always sure to find her curled up in the newest armchair or on the piece of stuff that best set off her swansdown coat. She spent endless time at her toilet; every morning she carefully smoothed out her fur. She used her paws to wash herself, and every single hair of her fur, having been brushed out with her rosy tongue, shone like brand-new silver. If anyone touched her, she at once removed the traces of the touch, for she could not bear to be rumpled. Her elegance and stylishness suggested that she was an aristocrat, and among her own kind she must have been a duchess at the very least. She delighted in perfumes, stuck her little nose into bouquets, and bit with little spasms of pleasure at handkerchiefs on which scent had been put; she walked upon the dressing-table among the scent bottles, smelling the stoppers, and if she had been allowed to do so would no doubt have used powder. She was Séraphita, and never did a cat bear a poetic name more worthily.

Théophile Gautier

Jess

The Cat as Teacher

We may learn some useful lessons from Cats, as indeed, from all animals. Cats may teach us patience, and perseverance, and earnest concentration of mind on a desired object, as they watch for hours together by a mousehole, or in ambush for a bird. In their nicely calculated springs, we are taught neither to come short through want of mercy, or go beyond the mark in its excess. In their delicate walking amidst the fragile articles on a table or mantelpiece, is illustrated the tact and discrimination by which we should thread rather than force our way and, in pursuit of our own ends, avoid the injuring of others. In their noiseless tread and stealthy movements, we are reminded of the frequent importance of secrecy and caution prior to action, while their promptitude at the right moment, warns us, on the other hand, against the evils of irresolution and delay. The curiosity with which they spy into all places, and the thorough smelling which any new object invariably receives from them, commends to us the pursuit of knowledge, even under difficulties. Cats, however, will never smell the same thing twice over, thereby showing a retentive as well as an acquiring faculty.

Then to speak of what may be learned from their mere form and ordinary motions, so full of beauty and gracefulness. What cat was ever awkward or clumsy?

Whether in play or in earnest, Cats are the very embodiment of elegance. As your cat rubs her head against something you offer her, which she either does not fancy or does not want, she instructs you that there is a gracious mode of refusing a thing; and as she sits up like a bear, on her hind legs, to ask for something, you may see the advantage of a winning and engaging way, as well when you are seeking a favour as when you think fit to decline one. If true courtesy and considerateness should prevent you not merely from positively hurting another but also from purposely clashing, say, with another's fancies, peculiarities, or predilections, this, too, may be learned from the cat, who does not like to be rubbed the wrong way (who does like to be rubbed the wrong way?), and who objects to your treading on her tail. Nor is the soft foot, with its skilfully sheathed and ever sharp claws, without a moral, too; for whilst there is nothing commendable in any thing approaching to spite, passion, or revenge, a character that is all softness is certainly defective. The velvety paw is all very well, but it will be the better appreciated when it is known that it carries within it something that is not soft, and which can make itself felt, and sharply felt, on occasion.

E. V. Lucas

Regent's Park Cats

London can fairly be described as a city of cats. I suppose there are more cats in London than in any other town in the world. Certainly there are more kinds of cats; from the silky, long-haired Persians and aristocratic Siamese to the common-and-garden tabbies who may be seen from morning to night sitting complacently on walls in the suburbs, outside shops, in offices, under fruit stalls, in fact in every place where there is room for a cat to observe and meditate. Some districts seem to be more thickly populated with cats than others. Regent's Park, where I live, is full of them. I am greeted every morning, on my three minutes' walk from Gloucester Gate to Camden Town station, by at least six friendly cats at different points on the road. If I am pressed for time, they are mildly reproachful; one bright-eyed tabby will follow me along the wall, bounding gracefully over gates and brick pillars, until I stop, as I always have to, and rub between his ears and under his chin. And for every cat I know and who knows me there are at least a score about in the few hundred yards which separate my house from the station, some on their lawful occasions, most of them just taking the air as they are accustomed. My Minna Minna Mowbray knows perfectly well that I hold conversations with other cats as soon as I get round the corner. One morning she followed me to the end of the terrace, where I was at once greeted by the bright eyed tabby. Apparently he is not admitted to Minna's social circle (being too clean and respectable, I can only assume) and Minna turned tail very haughtily. Since then she has pretended not to know that I am on speaking terms with other cats in the neighbourhood.

Michael Joseph

Harrison

A Visit to the First Cat Show, 1871

On the day for judging, at Ludgate Hill I took a ticket and the train for the Crystal Palace. Sitting alone in the comfortable cushioned compartment of a 'first class', I confess I felt somewhat more than anxious as to the issue of the experiment. What would it be like? Would there be many cats? How many? How would the animals comport themselves in their cages? Would they sulk or cry for liberty, refuse all food? Or settle down and take the situation quietly and resignedly, or give way to terror? I could in no way picture to myself the scene; it was all so new. Presently, and while I was musing on the subject, the door was opened and a friend got in. 'Ah!' said he, 'how are you?' 'Tolerably well,' said I; 'I am on my way to the Cat Show.' 'What!' said my friend, 'that surpasses everything! A show of cats! Why I hate the things; I drive them off the premises when I see them. You'll have a fine bother with them in their cages. Or are they to be tied up? Any how what a noise there will be, and how they will clutch at the bars and try to get out, or they will strangle themselves with their chains.' 'I am sorry, very sorry' said I, 'that you do not like cats. For my part, I think them extremely beautiful, also very graceful in all their actions, and they are quite as domestic in their habits as dogs, if not more so. They are very useful in catching rats and mice; they are not deficient in sense; they will jump up at doors to push up latches with their paws. I have known them knock at a door by the knocker when wanting admittance. They know Sunday from the week-day, and do not go out to wait for the meat barrow on that day; they—' 'Stop' said my friend, 'I see you do like cats, and I do not, so let the matter drop.' 'No' said I 'not so. That is why I instituted this cat show; I wish every one to see how beautiful a well-cared for cat is, and how docile, gentle, and may I use the term? – cossetty. Why should not the cat that sits purring in front of us before the fire be an object of interest, and be selected for its colour, marking and form? Now come with me, my dear old friend, and see the first Cat Show.'

Inside the Crystal Palace stood my friend and I. Instead of the noise and struggles to escape, there lay the cats in their different pens, reclining on crimson cushions, making no sound save now and then a homely purring, as from time to time they lapped the nice new milk provided for them. Yes, there they were, big cats, very big cats, middling sized cats, and small cats, cats of all colours and markings, and beautiful pure white Persian cats; and as we passed down the front of the cages I saw that my friend became interested; presently he said 'What a beauty this is! and here's another!' 'And no doubt,' said I, 'many of the cats you have seen before would be quite as beautiful if they were as well cared for, or at least cared for at all; generally they are driven about and ill-fed, and often ill-used, simply for the reason that they are cats, and for no other. Yet I feel a great pleasure in telling you the show would have been much larger were it not for the difficulty of inducing owners to send their pets from home, though you see the great care that is taken of them.' 'Well, I had no idea there was such a variety of form, size and colour,' said my friend, and departed. A few months after, I called on him; he was at luncheon, with two cats on a chair beside him – pets I should say, from their appearance.

Harrison Weir

Tiffany Tortoiseshell & Penny Black

Deberny & Peignot   *Yoko* ▶

Nine Lives

The house-cat is a four-legged quadruped, the legs as usual being at the corners. It is what is sometimes called a tame animal, though it feeds on mice and birds of prey. Its colours are striped, it does not bark, but breathes through its nose instead of its mouth. Cats also mow, which you all have heard. Cats have nine liveses, but which is seldom wanted in this country, coz' of Christianity. Cats eat meat and most anythink speshuelly where you can't afford. That is all about cats.

A schoolboy's essay 1903

Leman

Fortnum

Morning

*L*ong before the alarm goes I become aware of a warm heavy lump on the bed. It is Scamper. Slowly, as he senses I am coming awake, and very softly at first, he begins to purr. I reach out and press the button on the alarm; I don't think I shall be needing it today.

As the purr gets stronger I sense movement, first a slow curl into a ball and then the unwind to a full stretch. Soon he will climb over from his sleeping position in the small of my back to one where, lying close along my front, he stretches out both paws and presses them gently on my chin. At this range his purr seems to vibrate the bed. The touch of those soft pads makes it hard to believe this is the Great Ealing Hunter who last week brought in two small Squirrels as an offering.

The paws are retrieved and he edges up to press noses. I should have left the alarm set. It's going to be impossible to refuse him a cuddle and I shall be late again.

Tom Clapham

Morris

Doors, Cats and People, by a Cat

Doors are a problem in any house you will ever live in, and you simply have to learn to cope with them, or rather, with your people, and teach them the necessity of dropping whatever they happen to be doing to open one of them to let you in or out.

If you are fortunate you will have taken over a family both sufficiently cat-minded as well as ingenious to rig up one of those patent affairs cut into the bottom of the front door, which enables us to come and go as we please.

This, of course, is ideal for everyone, particularly for us, and enables us to go out at night without a lot of questions or admonitions. However, this does not solve the problem of inside doors, the ones to rooms, closets, cupboards, cellars, attics, etc., and the rule is that they must be left open at all times. You may have some difficulty with those leading from one room into another, or connecting with hallways, since the male of the family will be shouting about draughts, but there is no reason whatsoever why closet or cupboard doors should be kept shut.

You can learn very quickly how to open a door yourself, particularly if it is of the bent-handle kind, which you can work merely by getting up on your hind legs and putting your weight upon it. The round, doorknob handle is somewhat more of a problem, but when you have your full growth and weight you will find that by pushing or pulling on it you can get it to turn sufficiently to slip the latch.

However, when you have learned these tricks, don't under any circumstances let your family know that you have. It is their business and absolute concern to open and shut doors for you at any time, and your own little skill you will keep to yourself, for use at such times as when you may suddenly find yourself shut in a cupboard or when, for some reason or other, you are forbidden to go out.

To come in from the outside, scratching on the door and a good, loud miaow will alert someone. For an inside job, if your people are properly conditioned, it will be necessary to do no more than to go and sit by the door and just look at it. If that doesn't work pretty soon, you turn and look at them. If they are busy doing something give your miaow that they have come to connect with impatience. Whichever, remember that once you have attracted their attention to the fact that you want to get out, never let them go back to what they were doing. In any well-regulated household you come first.

Paul Gallico

Country Cat

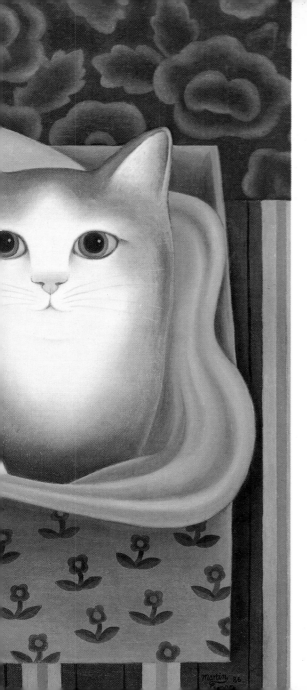

Gertrude Jekyll and her Cats

This feline menagerie played an important part in her domestic economy, and deserves more than passing notice. They began with four or five, and soon ran into double figures; there was a period within the writer's recollection when a visitor, on entering the sitting-room, would experience the sensations of those defeated in a game of musical chairs; whichever one he attempted to occupy, he found himself forestalled by a spreading matronly form, which proclaimed the imminence of yet another family. If, on the other hand, he was lucky enough to find a chair unoccupied he was soon to discover that Gertrude's attention, like Caesar's Gaul, was divided into three parts, one for himself, one for the tea-things, and one for Pinkieboy or Tittlebat, whose desire for company was not to be satisfied by a perfunctory caress. Her love of cats was, indeed, no passing fancy; it proceeded from a fundamental sympathy, a common attitude to the outside world. Like them she preserved a core of independence, she guarded an inviolable frontier which none might cross. Intolerant of dogs, whose barking exasperated her, she found in her 'pussies' that perfect satisfaction and companionship which human beings could so seldom be relied on to give her.

Francis Jekyll

Home Sweet Home

As Many Lives as a Cat

A cat rolled up into a ball, or crouched with its paws folded underneath it, seems an emblem of repose and contentment. There is something soothing in the mere sight of it. It may remind one of the placid countenance and calm response with which the sphinx seems to look forth, from the shadow of the Pyramids, on the changes and troubles of the world. This leads to the remark, that Cats after all are very enigmatical creatures. You never get to the bottom of cats. You will never find any two, well known to you, that do not offer marked diversities in ways and dispositions; and, in general, the combination they exhibit of activity and repose, and the rapidity with which they pass from the one to the other, their gentle aspects and fragile form, united with strength and pliancy, their sudden appearances and disappearances, their tenacity of life, and many escapes from danger ('as many lives as a Cat'), their silent and rapid movements, their sometimes unaccountable gatherings, and strange noises at night – all contribute to invest them with a mysterious fascination, which reaches its culminating point in the (not very frequent) case of a completely black cat.

C. H. Ross

Peace on Earth

Cats and Colours

I have also come across an instance of a white blue eyed Persian cat which had a strong affection for the blossom of the pink sweet-pea, and would jump on the table to search vases of flowers for her favourite morsel – often with disastrous results. Later on this same cat found rows of sweet-peas in a walled garden and her industry became unbounded. If pink sweet-peas were not to be had, she would eat other light-coloured flowers of that species, but never the dark ones, nor would she touch any other flower.

A Chair of your Own and How to Achieve it

*Y*ou will wish from the beginning, after you have once established your occupancy in the household you have chosen, to select and pre-empt a certain chair for your very own, not to be used thereafter by any other member of the family and to be reserved for your use whether you need or want it then or not.

The appropriation and holding of a chair takes time, vigilance, and patience, particularly if it happens at one time to have belonged to the so-called master of the house, or stands in such a position as to be used for practical purposes, say at a desk or table, or is meant for the convenience of visitors.

To begin with, in taking the chair over for your own exclusive use, you must be prepared at first to spend a great deal of time in it, curled up sleeping, or pretending to sleep even if you are not, in order that the family accustom themselves to seeing you there. People, as you will learn, are creatures of habit and extraordinarily lazy. They can be brainwashed into believing anything and eyewashed into accepting certain situations as *fait accompli*. By eyewashing I mean *seeing* you there on the chair every day, they will soon be convinced that it is 'your' chair and not 'their' chair.

However, this is still a preliminary stage of the campaign, and will result in no more than their refraining from making you leave it once you are there. It won't keep them from using it in your absence, or if you happen not to be in it.

The next stage consists of training them to keep out of it, which calls for a week or so of great watchfulness. You will remain in the vicinity of the chair, and when anyone appears to be heading for it, you will jump up and get there first. Having arrived there, you can do one of two things to hold the position: begin washing actively, above all being careful never to catch the eye of the person who has been trying for your place, or curling up and settling yourself in a sleeping position. If the latter, you will find it most convenient to your purpose to assume either a graceful or a 'cute' pose, such as placing one paw over your nose, or lying on your back with your feet hanging limply. The object here, and it will succeed in nine cases out of ten, is to distract the person's attention from his original idea, which was to sit down in the chair. If the pose is quaint enough, other members of the family will be brought to have a look, and they may even go to fetch a camera. If they still want to sit down, they will select another chair, and possession of yours will have been impressed even more deeply into their malleable brains.

Paul Gallico

Snowdrop

The Master's Cat

As the kittens grew older they became more and more frolicsome, swarming up the curtains, playing about on the writing table and scampering behind the bookshelves. But they were never complained of and lived happily in the study until the time came for finding them other homes. One of these kittens was kept, who, as he was quite deaf, was unnamed, and became known by the servants as 'the master's cat', because of his devotion to my father. He was always with him, and used to follow him about the garden like a dog, and sit with him while he wrote. One evening we were all, except father, going to a ball, and when we started, left 'the master' and his cat in the drawing-room together. 'The master' was reading at a small table; suddenly the candle went out. My father, who was much interested in his book, relighted the candle, stroked the cat, who was looking at him pathetically he noticed, and continued his reading. A few minutes later, as the light became dim, he looked up just in time to see puss deliberately put out the candle with his paw, and then look appealingly at him. This second and unmistakable hint was not disregarded, and puss was given the petting he craved. Father was full of this anecdote when all met at breakfast the next morning.

An incident described
by Charles Dickens' daughter Mamie

Polly

Minna Minna Mowbray

Of all my cats, past and present, Minna Minna Mowbray is the outstanding personality. Except to a connoisseur of cats Minna is not physically impressive. She is a short-haired tortoiseshell tabby, with tiny white paws to match her piquant white face. Her head is small but beautifully shaped. The rather large ears are grey, and streaks of orange fur run down between her amber eyes and on either side to the underpart of her delicate jaw, forming a regularly designed tortoiseshell frame for her white face. A flash of coral pink is visible when she opens her dainty mouth. Her teeth are white and strong. The underpart of her body is pure white and even in the soot and grime of London this is nearly always spotlessly clean. At kitten time it is dazzlingly white. This part of her is domestically known as her 'ermine'. When she is feeling particularly sociable, certain favoured members of the household are permitted, sometimes even encouraged, to massage it gently.

Minna is small, as cats go, but exquisitely proportioned. All her movements are graceful. She sits upright, with her tiny forepaws close together, her long, rather full tail coiled round. Her favourite position for sleep is a crouch, the hind legs drawn up close and head resting on the outstretched forepaws which she converts into cushions by turning them inwards. Sometimes she prefers to lie on her side, legs outstretched luxuriously at queer angles. Various attitudes we have come to recognise as meditative (often assumed, this one), ecstatic, proud (both these when kittens are on view), majestically indignant (accompanied by business with tail), enquiring (as when she wants to know what I am eating – this is primarily curiosity, for as often as not she will reject after close scrutiny the morsel I offer her) and leave-me-alone-please. This last is indicated by a haughty turning aside of her head; if this fails she will calmly turn her back, and if that gesture has no effect she will walk off with the air of an offended dowager.

Michael Joseph

Amish Cat

Concerning Mews both Conversational and Utilitarian

M stands for mew.

Mews may be divided into three classes:

1. The sad mew
2. The conversational mew
3. The utilitarian mew.

There are several sub-divisions of these main categories. We will deal with them in due course.

1. Concerning the sad mew, we will not write, for these are meant to be happy pages, where we can, at least for a while, forget the sorrows of the world. All the fears and bewilderments of the little helpless creatures of the animal kingdom are reflected in the mew of a kitten that is lost. In real life we would not pass on, but here, we may.

2. The conversational mew is heard to its best advantage on a summer evening, when the cat is at the far end of the lawn and suddenly sees his master approaching. Whereupon the cat turns and begins to walk towards his master. As he walks, he talks. Needless to say, there are many pauses in this progress, for there are patches of grass to be sniffed, and fallen leaves to be inspected; but as soon as these duties are performed, the promenade is resumed . . . always to the accompaniment of conversation. This is a sort of feline small talk; if it were translated it would probably be found to consist in comments on the weather, the extraordinary behaviour of the hedgehog under the copper beech, and the callousness of the gardener, whose weed-killer stings the paws. To which one would retort that it is better for pussy's paws to tingle for a few minutes than for pussy to be poisoned.

3. The utilitarian mew is most commonly heard outside closed doors. Even, I regret to say, outside some of the doors in my own house. For though there is a cat-door from the garden into my kitchen, and another cat-door from the kitchen into the dining-room, one cannot have cat-doors in every room.

Mews outside doors, it need hardly be said, should be instantly obeyed by cat-owners. How would the average human feel if every time he wished to leave the room he was obliged to sit on a mat and mew? However, lest it be assumed that we are carrying courtesy to extremes, we will admit that there are moments when, having opened a door for pussy, we have wished pussy would make up her mind as to whether she wants to go in or out. Only too often pussy remains poised half way, tail twitching, staring down the corridor, so that one cannot shut the door without endangering the tail. I have never been able to make up my mind whether it is permissible on such occasions to give pussy a slight prod. I admit that I have sometimes done this, but always at the cost of remorse.

Beverley Nichols

Gilbey

Acknowledgements

We would like to thank the following for permission to use extracts:

The Antique Collectors Club and the Estate of Gertrude Jekyll for 'Tittlebat and Tavy' from *Children and Gardens* by Gertrude Jekyll.

Hugh Michael Joseph for 'My cats', 'Regent's Park cats' and 'Minna Minna Mowbray' from *Cats Company* by Michael Joseph.

Penguin Books Ltd for 'Beatrix Potter's Journal' abridged by Glen Cavaliero and published by Viking Books, copyright Frederick Warne.

Michael Joseph Ltd for 'Séraphita' by Théophile Gautier and 'The Master's Cat' from *A Dictionary of Cat Lovers* by Christabel Aberconway.

Tom Clapham for 'Morning'.

William Heinemann Ltd for 'Doors' and 'The Chair' from *The Silent Miaow* by Paul Gallico.

Eric Glass Ltd for 'Concerning Mews' from *Cat's ABC and XYZ* by Beverley Nichols.

The editor and publisher apologise for any omissions and would be pleased to hear from those whom they were unable to trace.